Successful
Presentation
in a week

MALCOLM PEEL

ghton

ADLINE GROUP

the Institute of Management

FOUNDATION

The Institute of Management (IM) exists to promote the development, exercise and recognition of professional management.
The Institute embraces all levels of management from student to chief executive and supports its own Foundation which provides a unique portfolio of services for all managers, enabling them to develop skills and achieve management excellence.

For information on the various levels and benefits of membership, please write to:

Department HS
Institute of Management
Cottingham Road
Corby
Northants NN17 1TT
Tel: 01536 204222
Fax: 01536 201651

This series is commissioned by the Institute of Management Foundation.

Order queries; please contact Bookpoint Ltd, 39 Milton Park, Abingdon, Oxon OX14 4TD. Telephone: (44) 01235 400414, Fax: (44) 01235 400454. Lines are open from 9.00 - 6.00, Monday to Saturday, with a 24 hour message answering service. Email address: orders@bookpoint.co.uk

British Library Cataloguing in Publication Data
A catalogue record for this title is available from the British Library

ISBN 0 340 70544 2

First published 1992
Reprinted five times
Second edition 1998

Impression number 10 9 8 7 6 5 4 3 2 1
Year 2003 2002 2001 2000 1999 1998

Copyright © 1992, 1998 Malcolm Peel

Typeset by Multiplex Techniques Ltd, St Mary Cray, Kent
Printed for Hodder & Stoughton Educational, a division of Hodder Headline Plc, 338 Euston Road, London NW1 3BH
by Cox & Wyman Ltd., Reading.

CONTENTS

■ I N T R O D U C T I O N ■

Speaking in public worries almost everyone, even those who must do it regularly as part of their job or leisure activities.

People worry about such things as 'making a fool of myself', 'drying up', 'not finding the right word', 'not knowing what to do with my hands'. But the real problem is the worry itself, not the form it takes.

By following a few simple steps, we can improve our performance as public speakers, reduce our anxieties and discover that public presentation can be not only deeply satisfying, but even great fun.

We shall look at one step each day of the week. The steps are:

The steps to successful presentation

Sunday	– Basic preparation
Monday	– Producing content and structure
Tuesday	– Choosing and preparing aids
Wednesday	– Final preparations
Thursday	– Facing nerves
Friday	– Making the presentation
Saturday	– Handling questions

If you are committed to a presentation in the immediate future (maybe the very day you buy this book!) then turn first to pp. 61-96.

Basic preparation

The key to successful presentation is good preparation.
Today, we will look at the basics:

> *Basic preparation*
>
> - Analysing the occasion
> - Profiling the audience
> - Learning about the location
> - Defining our aim and objectives

Occasionally, we may be called on to speak with little or no
notice – perhaps to reply to a welcome or give a vote of
thanks, perhaps to step in when the intended speaker has
failed to arrive, or perhaps to state our viewpoint at a critical
stage of a meeting. Thankfully, for most of us, this is rare.

Usually we know that we must speak some time – from days to months – in advance. This period is precious, for it enables us to prepare, and preparation is a main key to success. The problems most of us feel when called upon to speak can be eliminated, or at least reduced, by thorough preparation.

However much (or little) time we have, preparation must begin with analysis of:

- the occasion on which we will be a speaker
- the audience that is expected
- the location at which it is to take place

This analysis may not necessarily be time-consuming – sometimes it may only take a minute or two – but it is the foundation for success.

Analysing the occasion

'Public speaking' and 'oral presentation' are descriptions which cover an enormous range of activities. At one end of the scale, we may be presenting the monthly accounts of our club to a committee of four or five people gathered in a sitting room. At the other end, we may be making a speech to a major conference in front of an audience of thousands, complete with TV cameras and the press.

For most of us, the occasion will fall somewhere in between. We may be making sales presentations, giving talks to clubs or societies, addressing meetings or perhaps giving training sessions.

The basic approach to oral presentation and public speaking is the same, whichever sort of occasion it is. However, the type and quantity of material, the aids and methods we choose and the level at which we present it will depend on the nature of the occasion; we must learn as much as we can about this in advance.

Our success will depend on how closely we match the expectations of the organiser and the audience. We must know what ground we are expected to cover, how long we should speak, and how we will fit in with other speakers and elements in the event.

The starting point for our analysis will be to ask whoever invited us to speak unless, of course, we are planning the event ourselves. If the event is a regular one, we may be able to get information from people who have attended previously.

Here is a checklist for analysing the occasion:

Analysing the occasion

- Which organisation is holding the event?
- What are the objectives of this organisation?
- What is the nature of the occasion?
- How formal is it to be?
- Why have I been asked? What is expected of me?
- Are there to be other speakers? If so, who? What are their subjects? Will they speak before or after me? Is it to be a team presentation?
- How long have I got? When will I start?
- Will there be questions? Discussion? A panel?
- Will there be a Chair for my session?
- What clothes are appropriate? How should I dress?

Profiling the audience

The key to success in any presentation is to please and satisfy our audience. It is they, not us, who must be the centre of the event. To analyse an audience which has not yet assembled is not easy, but we must try.

Few things are worse for a speaker than to arrive expecting a small group of friends and colleagues and to be confronted with an audience of hundreds, or to believe he is to address a packed audience of distinguished academics and find he is faced with half a dozen first-year students.

We must make the best estimate we can of the number of people who will be present. This will affect the kind of aids that are appropriate and the style we adopt. Major surprises on the day (whether too many or too few) are also bad for the morale.

The level of expertise of the audience is very important. Presentations which are pitched at the wrong level – either too high or too low – are sure to fail.

It will help if we can find out whether our audience is likely to hold any strong opinions about our subject; whether they have any biasses or preconceptions. Audiences usually feel neutral towards a speaker at the start of a presentation; but if there is any reason why they might be specially hostile or friendly we would do well to be warned.

The more we know about any inter-personal or inter-group tensions within the audience the better. Some people will be influential, others not. To appear to side with one faction may do little good if we thoroughly upset another.

As with the occasion, finding out about the expected audience usually requires us to speak to the organiser of the event (if it is not us), and if it is a regular one, to people who have been before.

Here is a checklist for audience analysis:

Profiling the audience

- How many are expected?
- Why will they be there?
- How knowledgeable will they be in the subject area?
- Will they have strong preconceptions or biasses about the subject? Might they be particularly friendly or hostile to me or to what I want to say?
- Will they be there in their own right, or representing others?
- Might there be tensions or conflicts within the audience? If so, what, and between whom?
- Who will be the key figures?

... ON ANIMAL LIBERATION

Learning about the location

The place in which a presentation is given can have a big effect on its success.

Size may be critical. Nothing will kill an event more quickly than for it to be held in a room which is much too big. Distractions can also be very damaging.

If we do not know what facilities are available or how to use them, we may lose an opportunity to impress, or, even worse, get tangled in embarrassing problems. The equipment available to help a speaker varies enormously. We cannot leave this to chance. To arrive with a set of magnificent 35mm slides, for example, and find there is no projector would probably destroy our presentation.

It is always helpful to visit the facility in which the presentation is to be made at an early stage if we can. If we are really lucky, we may be able to rehearse there.

Here is a checklist for learning about the location:

The location

- How do I get there?
- How long will it take? Are there any possible causes of delay? Is there convenient car-parking or public transport?
- Is the setting formal or informal?
- Will I be expected to speak from a platform?
- Is there a podium, rostrum or table?
- How is the audience seating arranged?
- What are the acoustics like?
- Is there public address equipment? If so, what kind of microphone? Who controls the volume? Does it work well?
- What are the visual aid facilities? If there is a 35mm projector, how are slides changed and will it take the same kind of magazine as mine?
- What format is the video? Where are the power points? Is there a flipchart, stand and markers?
- How are the visual aids placed relative to the audience? Where will I need to stand, and where can my aids be put before and after use?

Defining our aim and objectives

The more clearly we perceive what we want to achieve in a speech or presentation, the more likely we are to succeed. We must think hard and carefully in advance, and define our aim and objectives as accurately as we can. It is useful to write them down – this helps us to think clearly, creates a record to which we can refer and enables us, if we wish, to share them with the audience before we begin.

Our audience will have objectives too. They may have assembled specially in order to hear what we have to tell them, but even so, they will only be prepared to give their time and attention to us as long as they believe that we know what we are doing, why we are doing it, and what response we would like from it.

The aim

Our aim is the overall target we wish to reach with our presentation – the reason why we are planning to stand there and hold forth.

In some cases, the aim may be clear and self-explanatory. However, surprisingly often, there may be doubt. We may have been asked, for example, to speak at a conference on a subject in which we are an expert – but why? Are we there to give a general introduction to laypeople, to describe the findings of our latest research to experts, or to engage in a dialogue in a controversial area?

Our aim

We might, for example, decide that our aim was:

- 'To persuade the directors of the XYZ company to use the services of our organisation'

or

- 'To ensure that all members of the golf club understand why the subscription must rise by 50%'

or

- 'To entertain and amuse the dining club and help them to feel the annual dinner was a successful and enjoyable occasion'

or

- 'To improve the cold-calling performance of the sales representatives in my team'

and so on.

The objectives

Our objectives are the more detailed and precise steps we plan to take to reach our aim; not the methods we will use – those will come later – but the components included within the overall aim. Apart from conveying certain information, are we intending to convince, amuse, sell a product or ourselves, obtain immediate action, or what?

Negative objectives
Occasionally we may feel the need to include negative objectives – aspects we intend to avoid. We may wish to hide facets of our subject which are commercially secret. We may wish to avoid areas of controversy, or perhaps angles which might divert the attention of the audience from our main message. There may be parts of our case or members of our team we feel are weak. We may wish to avoid upsetting or offending some or all of our audience in a particular way.

Our objectives
For example, if our aim was: 'To persuade the directors of the XYZ company to use the services of our organisation',

we might decide that our objectives were:

- To convince them that each individual in our team is a qualified and experienced professional
- To demonstrate that our organisation has had relevant experience and satisfied other clients
- To show that we have the capacity to undertake the work they require within the timescale
- To establish good personal relationships between their senior management and our team
- To explain our fee structure and establish a basis for negotiation

The negative objectives might include:

- To hide as far as possible the failure of the contract with the ABC company
- To avoid a clear statement on price until our next wage negotiations have been completed

Personal or 'hidden' objectives
There may also be strictly personal objectives, such as:

Personal objectives

- To demonstrate to the new marketing director that I am a highly efficient member of staff
- To gain the commission which these sales would entitle me to and win the monthly sales award

There is nothing wrong with such objectives, although we are less likely to want to commit them to paper. They will usually remain hidden and we must beware that we are not misled by such objectives into giving a presentation that is unhelpful or uninteresting to most of the audience.

Behavioural objectives
Throughout our preparation, we should try to put ourself in the audience's place. We should ask not 'What do I want to say?', but 'What do I want them to hear and believe?'. For this reason, it can be helpful to write down objectives in a form which expresses what we intend from the angle of the audience. These are sometimes called 'behavioural objectives' as they are based on the behaviour we would like to see from our audience after the presentation. Such an approach is particularly helpful for training presentations.

Thus, if our aim was 'To improve the cold-calling of the sales reps in my team' we could set objectives in the form:

Behavioural objectives

By the end of the presentation, the representatives will:

- Accept the need for substantial improvement in cold-calling performance
- Know the steps to achieve cold-calling success
- Have insight into their own cold-calling effectiveness and the areas in which they need to improve
- Have set improvement targets and be motivated to achieve them

Content

Following Sunday's work, we know what we are aiming at.
The next steps are to fill out the content of our presentation,
to gather (or select) our material and to give it structure.

Content and structure

- Gathering material
- Selecting material
- Structuring the presentation

Gathering material

Do we need to gather?
We may not need to gather material. If we have:

- given the same, or a similar presentation before
- written an article, report (or book!) on the subject
- recently completed research or a detailed study of the subject
- access to and permission to use our organisation's or someone else's material

then we may have quite enough. In this case, our need will be to select and check what we have. This is discussed in the next section (p. 24).

When should we gather?
We should begin gathering as soon as possible. Material gathered three months in advance of the presentation is far more valuable than the same material gathered three days before. The extra time gives us the opportunity to digest the material and make it part of our thought processes. We can reject it, question it or support it by further research and additional material. If we work at the last minute, all this is impossible – we will have to take it or leave it as we find it.

The key source
If we are not a subject expert, our first aim should be to locate a *key source*. This will be a book, article, report or person that can give us the framework for the remainder of our research. This is not to suggest ruthless plagiarism. Apart from any legal or moral considerations, we shall want to put our own stamp on anything we use; if we do not, we might as well

invite our audience to read the source and save everyone, including us, much time and effort. Encyclopedias are a natural key source for many subjects; even if we know a subject well, it is always worth looking it up.

Where to look
There are many sources of material. They include:

Sources of material

- Our own experience
- Colleagues, family and friends
- Books
- Journals, magazines and newspapers
- Electronic databases
- Original research

Our own experience
Far-and-away the richest source of material for any presentation is our own first-hand experience and personality. Audiences warm to this in a way they never will to reported knowledge or facts. However sophisticated or expert the audience, something that actually happened to us will have more interest and carry more authority than a dozen quotations from international experts. This is the advantage of the oral presentation – the audience can read the established wisdom in any library, but a face-to-face meeting allows them to grasp and evaluate the speaker's unique personality and experience.

Colleagues, family and friends
Provided they are not deadly rivals, or planning to attend our presentation to learn from us, working colleagues will often prove an excellent source of material. Most people are quite flattered to be asked to help in this way. If they do help, we should always acknowledge such help in the presentation.

We should never ignore the help partners, children, aunts, uncles and cousins may be able to offer. From secondary school onwards, children can prove goldmines of knowledge, if we are humble enough to ask them.

Books
Books are an obvious source of material, but we need to check that they are reasonably up-to-date. A few books have been written specifically to offer material for public speakers – funny stories, jokes, witticisms, quotations, and little-known facts. Most library staff are extremely helpful and pleased to point us in the right direction.

Journals, magazines and newspapers
Recent journal articles will be more up-to-date than most books, and besides giving us additional material will indicate what the latest thinking is and what people are interested in at the present time. There is also more chance of finding the off-beat idea or the little-known fact in a journal article than a book.

If we are likely to speak (or write) on a subject on a number of occasions, a scrapbook can be a tremendous help. Much is written and happens day-by-day that gets lost, even to the expert. A 50p scrapbook and a stick of adhesive can preserve it for us.

Electronic databases
There are thousands of electronically-held databases
worldwide. Many are privately owned, and we may have
access to some of these. Others are available on payment of a
fee. Some are available for nothing.

Access to most of these is by means of a personal computer,
telephone link and modem. If we do not possess the
necessary equipment or software our employer or a local
library may be able to help. The Internet is rapidly becoming
a major resource, if properly used.

Original research
It may be part of our job or we may have the facilities to
carry out original research to provide material for a
presentation. Usually, however, we shall have been asked to
give the presentation – perhaps in the form of a paper to a
learned body – because we are known to have already
carried out research. If this is the case, we are more likely to
need to *select* material than to gather it. This is discussed in
the second part of this chapter.

Organising the material
A good method of organising our material is to write the
headings of each of our main sections on the top of separate
sheets of paper. We can then either jot notes of our other
material on the appropriate sheets or, if we have a great deal
of material, endorse already-written notes with the section
numbers and place them in order in a folder or file.

Selecting material

Sooner or later, our task will be to stop gathering material and to select from what we have.

How much material?
The amount of material needed can be difficult to judge, especially if we are not a practised speaker. How much will become clearer as our work proceeds, both in the actual gathering and in the next step – structuring. Having established a structure, we may realise that we need to add more material to fill in a section or support an argument and there will always be some to-ing and fro-ing between these two steps. Occasionally our research may even indicate that our objectives were too ambitious or too limited, and we may need to go back and revise them.

Don't prepare too much

Because they are afraid of drying up, inexperienced speakers almost always prepare more material than they have time to use, however much time they have.

If we have any doubt on how long our material will last, we must check by careful rehearsal (Wednesday, p. 55).

Flexibility

Some speakers – especially when giving training sessions – give themselves greater flexibility by classifying their material in three ways:

- *core material* which is essential to the presentation
- *disposable material* (e.g. extra examples) which can be passed over without harming the message if time is short.
- *supplementary material* which can be used if there is time to spare, or in answering questions

Old material

It is comforting to have already existing material when we are preparing for a presentation; we or a colleague may have given a similar presentation before, and the notes and visual aids may have been kept.

But the temptation to pick the material up and use it without further examination must be resisted.

The dangers in using old material, whether our own or someone else's, include:

The dangers of old material

- It was prepared for a different audience
- The occasion and the speaker's objectives may have been different
- It may not have worked well last time
- It may not take account of lessons learnt during previous presentations
- It may not now be up-to-date

Structuring the presentation

Any form of communication – a report, an article, a letter, a book – needs a structure, but for an oral presentation, good structure is absolutely essential.

The benefits of a good structure
The audience has only one chance to understand what we are saying. If they lose the thread, they may never pick it up and even if they do, they may have missed vital points. A clear, simple structure is the best way of preventing this happening. With it, we can set up checkpoints and signposts which will help to keep the audience with us. If they do lose us, they can rejoin us comparatively easily at the next junction.

The benefits of structure

A good structure will:

- Attract attention
- Hold interest
- Help understanding
- Make our message more memorable

Types of structure

Three common types of structure are suitable for an oral presentation:

> ### Structures for a presentation
>
> • Logical argument
> • Narrative
> • Formal

Logical argument

All that we say should be logical. If it is not, we are in trouble. However, this does not mean that to follow one logical argument step by step from start to finish will necessarily provide a good structure for our presentation; this can be extremely tedious for the audience and may be inappropriate for our objectives.

A logical argument will be suitable as our structure if we are presenting a case to a court or tribunal, speaking in a formal debate or seeking to convince an audience of the truth of our opinion. In other situations, other structures are likely to be more effective.

Narrative structure
Everyone loves a good story. The narrative structure or storyline is the one most likely to grab and hold the attention of the audience and make what we say memorable. If we can structure what we want to say as a story, we are on to a winner. But to work, the story must meet three conditions:

A story must be

- Good
- Well-told
- Relevant to our objectives

Unfortunately, few business presentations can be structured
in this way as a whole. However, it is often possible to use
stories as part of the overall structure, as a separate section
or to make a particular point.

Formal structure
If neither the logical argument nor the storyline are suitable
for our presentation, we shall need to use a more formal
structure. Probably the oldest advice about structure is:

> 1   Tell them what you are going to
>   tell them
> 2   Tell them
> 3   Tell them what you have told them

This structure provides the essential elements of
introduction, main section and conclusion. The repetition, if
skilfully done, will help understanding and retention.The
introduction ('Tell them what you are going to tell them')
and the conclusion ('Tell them what you have told them')
will be prepared last. Both should be prepared with great
care, as they are the most important sections.

The introduction

If we are to command attention, especially in a large
gathering, we need to be larger than life – most openings
benefit from a touch of drama. Before the introductory
summary, the introduction should include something
designed to attract the attention, whet the appetite and focus
the audience's thinking. We need not go over the top, but
we should not be self-conscious. We should avoid spoiling

the effect by explanation or too many words. Having grabbed attention, we should maintain the suspense and only release it when we are ready to do so, ideally not before the conclusion.

Methods of grabbing attention include:

> ### Attention-grabbing starts with
>
> - Making a joke
> - Telling an anecdote
> - Making a controversial statement
> - Displaying a key visual aid
> - Performing an arresting action

attention - grabbing

Making a joke
A good joke will gain attention, establish empathy and focus the audience's thinking.

However, the joke must be funny, not too well known, relevant to our subject and well-told. To tell a joke which does not succeed will set us back; it is much better not to try. To tell one which has little or no connection with our subject will not get us further forward; we shall have to start all over again once the laughter has died down.

Unless we are an expert humorist, it is better to stick to good one-line jokes than risk a story of any length. If we have doubts, it is better to choose another method of starting.

Telling an anecdote
We may have a story which, whilst not being funny, grabs attention in other ways. It may be a story of deep human interest, preferably true and ideally which happened to us. Having engaged the audience's interest in this way, we can sometimes hold back the conclusion until the end of the presentation, thus holding their attention right through.

Making a controversial statement
Startling or provocative statements will attract and focus attention and whet the appetite of our audience in the same way as a headline in a newspaper.

For success, we must pick out something that we can explain and justify as we go on – an intriguing aspect, unexpected statistic or main conclusion from our message encapsulated in a pithy way. We must not blunt its edge by immediate explanation; our audience must wait for this, possibly until the end.

Displaying a key visual aid
To display a key visual aid, possibly in silence, can make an excellent start; a slide, foil or pre-prepared flipchart which summarises or focuses on a key aspect of our message. It

should be pictorial, preferably without words, bright, intriguing and simple. Producing an object such as a piece of machinery, equipment or clothing relevant to our subject will also focus attention in the same way.

As with the controversial statement, we should not explain it right away, explanation (or spontaneous enlightenment) will come as we proceed. An especially useful device is to produce an ohp foil to which we can add one or more explanatory overlays (see Tuesday, p. 39).

Performing an arresting action
We may start by performing some action relevant to our subject in mime or dumb show – a demonstration (particularly if there is an element of manual skill) or the manipulation of some machinery or equipment.

The opening summary
Having engaged the audience's attention, our next task is to 'Tell them what we are going to tell them': to lay out in summary form the structure of the presentation. This is best done with a visual aid – slide, foil or flipchart – listing the title and headings of our main sections. We should display it, read it through aloud, and put it on one side for use as we move from point to point or in the conclusion.

The main section

The main section ('Tell them') will need a number of main headings – usually between three and six. More and the structure will be too complicated for an audience to understand or remember. We may have one or two sub-headings within the main structure but, once again, there must not be too many or both we and our audience will lose our way. The main sections must follow smoothly in a meaningful order.

The conclusion

Like the end of a piece of music, we must leave our audience satisfied, and in no doubt that we have finished.

Concluding summary
If we are using a formal structure, we should conclude with a crisp, clear summary of our main points. This can be reinforced by displaying the summary with which we started.

We may follow the summary by:

Closing options

- Picking up the point we started the presentation with
- A challenge or call to action
- A question for the audience to think about
- A relevant witticism or good joke

Presentation aids

Having decided what we want to achieve and sorted out the content of our presentation, the next step is to choose our aids. The voice alone is not enough for success; there are many aids available to help us. The room in which the presentation will take place, its equipment and furniture, will also affect our success. Today, therefore, we will consider:

Presentation aids

- Why use aids?
- The dangers of aids
- Choosing aids
- The room

Why use aids?

Preparing and using aids requires extra work but it is
always worthwhile. Aids offer many benefits:

> *Presentation aids:*
>
> • Attract attention
> • Help understanding
> • Help retention
> • Give pleasure

Aids attract attention
The speaker's voice alone quickly loses attention, even when
skilfully used. By adding one or more other sense, aids wake
an audience up and focus their attention. In a presentation
of any length, the variety alone helps to rekindle and hold
flagging attention.

Aids help understanding
Words are often not the most efficient way to convey
messages. The nature of an unfamiliar object will be far better
understood if we see a picture; better still if we are able to
touch it. The layout of a building or a tract of country will be
best conveyed by a plan or map. Relationships within an
organisation are much clearer if shown in the form of a chart.
The meaning of statistics is far easier to grasp from a graph.
Complex theories may be expressed by means of pictograms;
the working of a machine from a diagram.

Aids help retention

Words must be very startling or special to stick in the mind; the other senses are much more retentive. Most people remember things they have seen more readily than something they have heard. If they have touched and handled – perhaps even operated or used – something, they are even more likely to remember it.

Aids give pleasure

Almost everyone likes pictures. Well designed and produced aids give pleasure, especially if they make good use of colour.

The dangers of aids

We have all attended presentations which have been wrecked by aids. Endless sequences of slides filled with words; a video in the wrong format; a projector which broke down; slides in the wrong order, upside down and inside out. Above all, we have come from presentations remembering the wonderful technology used, but without a clue as to the message it was meant to convey.

Aids are not, therefore, automatically beneficial. To get the benefits and avoid the dangers we must follow a few simple guidelines.

Success with aids

Aids should:

- Reinforce the message
- Match the equipment available
- Be carefully prepared
- Not be too many
- Not be too complicated
- Be skilfully used

Choosing aids

There is an ever-growing range of presentation aids.
They include:

Aids to presentation

- Blank flipcharts and whiteboard
- Prepared flipcharts or posters
- Overhead projector
- Slide projector
- Videotape and film
- Multimedia and other electronic
  aids
- Models and samples
- Handouts

Blank flipcharts or whiteboard
Blank flipcharts are the most flexible and generally useful aid. They can be torn off and kept on display with masking tape or Blutac. However, they are not suitable for audiences of more than about thirty, or for formal presentations.

Whiteboards must only be used with the special dry markers, and cleaning can be a nuisance.

Prepared flipcharts or posters
Prepared flipcharts or posters can be produced in advance to a high, professional standard and used to display complicated material. However, they are only suitable for audiences of up to forty to fifty, are clumsy to carry around and soon get dog-eared.

Overhead projector (ohp)
The ohp is a versatile and useful aid which is widely available. Foils (also known as transparencies, acetates or vu-foils) can be pre-prepared or written during the presentation. Pre-prepared foils are easy to carry around and store for future use. The image can be projected at varying sizes, making them suitable for audiences of up to several hundred. An impressive technique is to produce foils which can be placed on top of one another – overlays – each adding information to those beneath. In this way a complete picture can be built up step-by-step as we speak.

There are drawbacks. We may come to rely too much on a set of foils and neglect the basic techniques of presentation. Also, some projectors have noisy fans and every so often a bulb will blow (although many projectors are now fitted with two).

Slide projector
The 35mm slide projector can project an image of variable size, making it suitable (with appropirate equipment) for very large audiences – even of thousands. Slides can be produced to a high professional standard and are fairly easy to store and carry around, especially if kept in a carousel.

Here too, there are dangers. Slides can be costly to produce, depending on the standard and the method used. As with ohp foils, there is the danger of relying too much on a set of slides and neglecting the other skills of presentation. Slides may get out of order, the wrong way round or upside down. Projection requires a darkened room, which limits contact between speaker and audience, especially if the speaker must operate the projector from the back of the room. If remote control is not available, two people are needed with a good system of communication.

By using several electronically linked projectors and sound equipment, tape-slide presentations can be developed with superimposed images, cross-fades and other special effects. Like the multimedia aids discussed later, these are very powerful, but can also be very dangerous aids.

For both foils and slides, there are three golden rules:

The golden rules

- **Don't use too many**; 8–10 are enough; more just confuse
- **Use plenty of graphic material**; pictures, charts, diagrams, maps, etc
- **Don't crowd too many words on**; 20–25 on a slide or foil is plenty

Videotape and film
Both have similar advantages and drawbacks:

Advantages of video
- Can demonstrate processes and events
- Is highly memorable
- Adds a professional touch

Drawbacks of video
- May take over the presentation
- May need the room to be darkened
- Equipment may malfunction

Probably the most effective use of film and video is in the display of short clips specially produced to reinforce the presenters message.

Multimedia and other electronic aids

There is an ever-growing and impressive range of electronic aids to presentation. These aids include:

> *Multimedia and other electronic aids*
>
> • Digital cameras
> • Computers
> • Full multimedia
> • Interactive keypads

Digital cameras

Like the almost forgotten epidiascope, these are used to project a magnified image of either two- or three-dimensional objects onto a screen. In this way, they have a highly-specialized but extremely useful function.

Computers

Computer-generated material (eg graphs, tables and spreadsheets) can be used directly during a presentation. If the computer is linked to a network, material can be provided from other computers, or from sources such as the Internet.

The screens of laptop or notebook computers can be used as an aid, but only with very small groups, all of whom can view the screen comfortably. LCD projection panels can be placed on top of an ohp and plugged into the computer, enabling the screen image to be magnified and projected for larger groups. Large-screen projectors enlarge to a much greater size, and are thus suitable for the largest audiences.

Full multimedia

'Multimedia' adds sound to the screen output of a computer, and may be arranged to use input from video or audiotape or CD-ROM. It thus provides an almost unlimited method for creating, blending and using textual, graphic and sound material from the widest variety of sources.

Interactive keypads

Members of an audience can be provided with keypads, enabling them to agree, disagree or react in other ways, with the results being immediately visible.

The range and power of electronic aids (especially of full multimedia) is, as we have said, growing rapidly, and offers both great advantages and serious dangers to the presenter.

Advantages of multimedia

- Highly impressive
- Almost limitless capability; text, graphics, sound (separately and in combination), still and moving images
- Direct input from a range of sources, including networks
- Flexible and can accept input during the presentation

Dangers of multimedia

- Comes between presenter and the audience
- Needs darkened room
- May appear too slick, especially for smaller audiences

- May be very expensive
- Complex to prepare and use
- Subject to rapid obsolescence

The best advice may be, therefore, to be aware of what multimedia can offer, but to use it only with the utmost care, bearing in mind the size and culture of the audience and the objectives of the presentation. We should never let machinery, however clever, stand between us, our message and personality and the audience.

Models and samples
Models of objects which cannot be displayed, such as machinery or buildings, can be a powerful aid with smaller groups.

Samples which can be handed round will use the senses of both sight and touch. If they can be manipulated in some way to demonstrate their use, they will give instant insight and be immensely memorable. Examples include samples of materials used in a process, components of a machine or the products beind discussed. If the sense of smell can be involved, as with food, drink and perfume, the ultimate aid will probably have been found.

Handouts
Handouts summarizing the main points of the presentation help understanding and retention. Unless there are special circumstances, they should always be given out at the end.

The room

The environment can make or break a presentation. There are several aspects we should consider:

> *The room*
>
> - Size
> - Acoustics
> - Noise levels
> - Distractions
> - Ventilation
> - Lighting
> - Furniture

Size

Nothing kills a presentation more certainly than a room which is much too small or much too big. If it is too small, people will be cramped, uncomfortable and may not be able to see and hear properly. If it is too big, the atmosphere will be cold, empty and may create a feeling of failure.

People may feel embarrassed and wonder what has gone wrong.

We (or the organisers) will have estimated how many people we expect. If, on the day, we find we have got it badly wrong, it is always right to consider before starting whether we can switch to another room. If not, and the room is too big, we can make it feel fuller by asking people to move up to the front before we start.

Acoustics

If public address (pa) equipment is available we should check it like the other equipment. If we have the slightest doubts about the acoustics we should ask whether everyone can hear us right at the start. It is not possible to check properly in advance as a room full of people has quite different acoustics from the same room when empty.

Noise level

There is a law of nature which says that whenever a presentation is being given someone nearby is repairing the central heating boiler, hammering nails into a wall or digging up the road with a pneumatic drill. There may not be a lot we can do about such events, but bribery has occasionally been known to work.

Distractions

Visual distractions can ruin a presentation. If anything particularly interesting (such as a busy street, office or public park) is visible through the windows, we may wish to re-arrange the seating so that it is behind the audience, or even draw the curtains.

Interruptions are a nuisance. If they are at all likely (as, for example, if we are meeting in someone's office) we should make use of any available aid to prevent them – a secretary or assistant outside or a notice on the door. Phones should, of course, be disconnected or diverted.

Ventilation

If the room is too hot and stuffy, our audience will get snoozy; if it is too cold, our listeners will get tense and unhappy. The choice is often between external noise or adequate ventilation; it is courteous to ask the audience to make it.

Lighting

Poor lighting creates an atmosphere of gloom. On the other hand, if the lighting is too bright, it will make ohps, slide projectors or videos harder to see. In particular, we should check that light is not falling directly on the screen. Sunlight upsets some people, especially if it is shining directly into their eyes.

Furniture

The furniture and its arrangement sets the style and feeling of the presentation. It can give a sense of formality or informality, of lecture, schoolroom or group discussion. It can enhance or spoil the use of our aids. We should never leave it to chance.

We should check that there are the right number of chairs, that they are neither too comfortable nor too spartan and that they are suitably arranged.

Desks/tables

If people will need papers, we should see that tables, desks or attachments to the chairs are available. Tables add formality to a meeting.

Final preparations

So far, we have defined exactly why we are speaking, obtained and selected our material, and chosen and prepared our aids. Before we finally take the stage, we must consider:

- Speaker's notes
- Rehearsal
- How to rehearse
- The rehearsal audience

Speaker's notes

Good notes give confidence and can do a great deal to minimise nerves. There are four basic approaches, and it is worth looking at the strengths and weaknesses of each:

Four approaches to speaker's notes

- No notes at all
- Use of visual aids as notes
- A full, verbatim script
- Prompt cards or sheets

No notes at all
A few speakers can spellbind an audience, speaking for maybe half an hour without a single note. To do this always creates a magnificent impression of competence and knowledge. People remember it for long afterwards – often far longer than they remember what was actually said.

However, this is not a sound model to follow at the start of our public speaking career. There is nothing to be ashamed of in using notes. Producing good speaker's notes is the best method of ensuring that we have structured our presentation properly; using them is the best protection against excessive nerves. If, as we gain experience, we discover a talent for noteless speaking, we can cultivate it , but this will come later – if at all – not now!

Use of visual aids as notes

Rather than preparing separate notes, some speakers use their visual aids as prompts. This can be done, for example, if we are using a set of overhead projector (ohp) foils or 35mm slides.

To use this approach, we must have all the material we need on the aids. This may not always be the case, and we should never prepare aids simply to act as notes. It is possible, if we use ohp foils with card frames, to add explanatory notes on the frames, but this can be confusing. As discussed on Tuesday, aids which have too many words on them do not work well, and a presentation consisting of slide after slide, each with lengthy text or lists of words, rapidly becomes boring.

It is best not to rely on aids as speaker's notes unless we are very familiar with our material and have become practised in presenting it. Under these conditions, the method can be effective.

Full, verbatim script
Some speakers write out, word-for-word, all they intend to say in the form of a script and then read it. But this approach has many drawbacks:

The drawbacks of a verbatim script

- Few people can write a script that sounds natural when read
- Few people can read a script so that it sounds natural
- A verbatim script is inflexible
- It is easy to lose one's place whilst reading
- It is impossible to read and maintain good audience contact

However, there are some situations in which producing a verbatim script can be justified:

> ### When a verbatim script may be justified
>
> * To write out and put aside
> * If we are on the record
> * If we are using an autocue
> * If someone writes our speech for us

To write out and put aside
There can occasionally be an advantage in the discipline of writing our script in full. It may help us to organise our thoughts and material and thus give additional assistance during preparation, especially with an important and formal presentation, or if we are covering unfamiliar ground.

If we are on the record
A leading statesman, diplomat or party leader may be on the record worldwide, and every word is likely to be analysed and dissected for possible shades of meaning. For such people, a verbatim script may be inevitable, although they are also likely to have the services of a professional speech writer to prepare it. Most of us will hardly ever be in such a position, although there are a few occasions – speeches announcing a major company policy (expansion, contraction, obtaining a big contract, etc.) – when it may be justified.

If we are speaking to a conference, or presenting a paper to a learned institution, we may also need a full script for publication later in the proceedings. In this case, writing it out first will kill two birds with one stone.

If we do decide, for whatever reason, to prepare a verbatim script, we should neither read it nor try to memorise it. The next step is to condense it into good speaker's notes of the kind described on page 54 ('Prompt cards or sheets'), put the script firmly aside and speak from our notes.

The autocue

There is a machine called an autocue or teleprompter which projects a rolling image of our script onto one or two transparent angled glass screens in front of our eyes. This is sometimes used at major events by speakers who are unsure of their speaking ability, or possibly need a full script for the kind of reasons mentioned above. For most speakers, the device has many drawbacks: it is expensive, needs a skilled operator and calls for much rehearsal by the speaker.

If someone writes our speech for us

If we are a prominent and busy person, we may have the services of someone to write our speech for us. However, we will still sound more convincing if we speak from good notes. We should ask the speech writer to prepare prompt cards as well as the script or, better still, prepare our own. The reading of prepared scripts is one reason why so many speeches by public figures are unimpressive.

Prompt cards or sheets

The commonest and best form for speaker's notes is a set of prompt cards or sheets. The use of cards, each containing notes for a main section or heading of a presentation, is almost a tradition amongst some speakers, although sheets of paper will achieve almost the same effect. Each has advantages.

Cards
They are easier to hold and more compact. They will not rustle and if our hands are trembling they will not amplify the movement as much as paper. Because they are smaller, they are less likely to be overloaded with detail.

Paper
It is easier to file, and can be typed or printed neatly, possibly using a word-processor or desktop publisher.

Whichever we use, the basic layout will be the same. Each card or sheet should have:

The layout of a prompt card or sheet

(A number to show the sequence)

- **A LARGE, VERY CLEAR MAIN HEADING**
  indicating the section of the presentation it covers
- **Not more than five or six clearly-written sub headings**
  (If necessary) figures, or a word or two to prompt points we wish to make: stories, examples or illustrations
- Prompts on when to use our aids
- Guides to timekeeping
  (Optional – some speakers find this helps, others do not)

The format of prompt cards or sheets reflects exactly the structure we have set up during the previous step (Monday, pp. 27-31), and producing them will act as a check that the structure is good and complete.

Rehearsal

Rehearsal is not always necessary and sometimes we just do not have the opportunity. However, it offers many benefits:

> *Rehearsal*
>
> - Reduces nerves
> - Improves performance
> - Helps judge timing
> - May help to refine the content

There are circumstances in which rehearsal is particularly important.

> *When rehearsal is important*
>
> - For team presentations
> - For particularly important presentations
> - If we plan to use unfamiliar aids
> - If we have unusual anxiety

Team presentations

Presentations using two or more presenters have special difficulties. Speakers may not understand how they are to work together and may leave gaps, duplicate or even contradict each other. For success, they will need to plan ahead:

Planning team presentations

Each presenter must:

- Agree who will cover which areas
- Know what opinions each will express, especially in controversial areas
- Plan the use of aids, and how each can help the other when using them
- Know the handover points and the cues for each
- Agree how questions and discussion are to be handled

All this makes at least one proper rehearsal essential.

Particularly important presentations

In one sense, every presentation is important. However there will always be some which, for whatever reason, have special significance. They may have a key role in selling, be aimed to impress a particularly important audience, or perhaps be part of a special occasion. If we are planning a presentation in this category, one or more rehearsals will always be justified.

Unfamiliar aids

Nothing will wreck a presentation more surely than bad use of aids. If our slides are in the wrong order or upside down, we block the screen from the audience, our foils or flipcharts are too small to read, or we can't operate the controls of the video, there is little chance of success. Thorough rehearsal is the best protection against all these dangers. If it can be arranged, rehearsal in the room and with the equipment for the actual presentation will be especially helpful.

Unusual anxiety

Speakers usually feel some anxiety about a presentation, but beyond a certain level anxiety can rise to panic. Rehearsal is one of the most effective methods of cutting anxiety back to size. It is particularly valuable if there is any specific problem on our mind – timing, perhaps, whether we can find the right words to express a particular point, or whether we can bring off the start or the conclusion we have planned.

How to rehearse

Take it seriously

To be worthwhile, rehearsal must be taken seriously. Surprisingly, some people feel more self-conscious rehearsing than giving the actual presentation. There is something about talking to an empty room or a video camera that can sound quite silly and this may result in our skipping bits, hurrying through or giving up halfway, none of which will help.

Timing

It is natural to check the timing during rehearsal. This is helpful, but we must remember that most rehearsals are much quicker than the real thing. Whilst there is no exact rule, the real presentation will probably take 25–50% longer than a rehearsal.

Apart from the total length of the presentation, we should check the time needed for each main section and note it on our prompt cards or sheets. In this way we can monitor how time is going and adjust before a crisis point is reached.

Location

If we have the opportunity to rehearse in the place where the presentation is to take place, we should grasp it. It will help enormously to get the feel of the place, and to learn how the table, lectern, ohp, screen and other furniture and equipment are placed. If we are unhappy with their arrangement and can move them, we should.

Over-rehearsal

It is possible to rehearse too much, so that we lose interest and spontaneity and become slick and unnatural. We must know when to stop.

Part-rehearsal

If we have not much time, it may be sensible to rehearse just part of a presentation; the start, conclusion or a key or difficult section. If we have plenty of time, extra rehearsal of the difficult bits will always help.

The rehearsal audience

Rehearsals are best if they give us some kind of feedback on how effective we have been and what points need attention. To achieve this, we need at least one of the following:

The rehearsal audience

- A live audience of colleagues
- A professional in presentation techniques
- Family or friends
- Video recording
- Audio recording
- A mirror

Colleagues
To rehearse in front of a live audience of two or three colleagues is usually the best choice, if it is practicable. However, to work, we must find people who are both reasonably good judges of subject and presentation and who are prepared to be honest and thorough in giving feedback.

A professional in presentation techniques
There are consultants who are prepared, for a suitable fee, to give professional advice in the presentation of specific speeches, arranging rehearsal and giving both verbal feedback and video replay.

Family or friends
We should not despise the value of rehearsing in front of non-experts. They can often pick out gaps or inconsistencies in what we plan to say, and may spot assumptions which are not justified or arguments which are not logical. Apart from this, they are more likely to be frank and honest with their comments than people who know us less well.

Video recording
Video recording, especially if combined with the comments of a live audience, provides the ultimate in efficient feedback.

Audio recording
This is a poor second-best to video, but still worth doing.

The mirror
The poor old mirror is better than nothing, but only just.

Nerves

Nerves are the biggest problem for most unpractised speakers. There is no cure, but many helpful things can be said. Today we will look at these.

> *Getting the better of nerves*
>
> - Why bother about them?
> - Facing our fears
> - Nerve-reducing tricks
> - Setting out our stall

Why bother about them?

The great day has dawned. We feel petrified and are considering ringing up the organiser to say that we have contracted the lurgi and are on the point of death. However, this would be sad after all the work we have put in, and would disappoint the many people who have been looking forward to hearing us for so long.

Everyone feels them

To feel nerves is completely normal. All good speakers are tense before giving a presentation and the same is true of actors, instrumentalists, singers and other performers. However experienced and successful, almost all will admit to nerves before going 'on stage'.

Nerves are helpful

The sense of tension and anticipation ensures that our adrenalin is flowing and this, in turn, will key us up for maximum performance. There is a far greater risk of failing if we feel no nerves at all than if the desire to succeed gets us keyed up.

They won't notice

Since our feelings are so obvious to us, we assume that everyone else must know about them. But it is hard to guess what is going on in someone else's head at the best of times, and at a distance of twenty feet in a crowded room it is nearly impossible. Unless we tell them, or do something to give the game away such as holding a sheaf of papers in a violently trembling hand, the chances are they will never notice.

They want us to succeed

If a speaker or other performer gets into difficulties, the
audience usually feels more embarrassment than the person
making the speech. For this reason, the audience will
normally do whatever they can to give a speaker any help
he or she needs. They will wait patiently, suggest words,
point out the page of notes which has been dropped or the
elusive switch on the ohp. Only if we have done something
to offend the audience might help not be forthcoming.

The value of preparation

It is no accident that we have not reached actually making
the presentation until today. If we have worked carefully
from Sunday to Wednesday our task today – facing our
audience at last – will be far less stressful.

In particular, well-prepared notes (Wednesday, p. 49) will
prove their worth at this point, available as a sort of life-
jacket if the waters get stormy. If we have also rehearsed
carefully (Wednesday, p. 56) this will do much to strengthen
our confidence.

Facing our fears

As with all irrational fears, it helps to face them squarely and ask 'What exactly am I afraid of?' In the case of speakers' nerves, there are several common answers:

What speakers fear

- Not coming up to the audience's expectations
- Making a fool of myself
- Drying up
- Not finding the right word

Not coming up to the audience's expectations
Giving an inadequate presentation is one of the commonest fears – the worry that we are not clever enough, do not know enough or have nothing to offer which can interest our audience.

Audience analysis was part of the first step (Sunday, p. 9) and if we have carried it out carefully we shall have a sound basis for knowing what they want and how we can satisfy them.

In fact, we will have been invited (if we have been invited) by people who were sure we had something to offer; the organisers will only have asked us if they were quite convinced we could do it and they have at least as much at stake as we do. If it was our own choice to speak, then we must have the courage of our original convictions.

Making a fool of myself
This is one of the most irrational fears, and therefore hard to quell. It is similar to the panic that grips some people when standing on the edge of a precipice. But just as hardly anyone actually jumps off, so our common sense and judgement will keep us safe in front of the audience.

If something does go wrong, it is the way we react, not what has happened, which matters. By remaining calm – adding a touch of humour if we can – an accident can be turned into a blessing. It will form a bond between us and the audience, show our common humanity and add a little light relief. It will also make our presentation much more memorable. Danger can only come if we allow ourself to show embarrassment or panic.

Drying up
If we have prepared properly and provided ourself with good notes, there can be little danger of drying up. We must also remember that there is nothing wrong with occasional silence. The speaker is not bound to keep up a continuous torrent of words; indeed, it is much better not to do so. An occasional pause to collect our thoughts, or find the right place in our notes, is entirely acceptable. Controlled silence actually serves to emphasise a point and give the audience time to reflect on the wise things we have said. If we have a carafe or bottle of water and a glass, we can use the legitimate ploy of pouring and sipping some. No one will object (as long as it is not done too often).

Not finding the right word
Speakers are most likely to dry up if they search too hard for the *mot juste*. But unlike writers, there is no need for speakers to strive for semantic perfection; to try one or two alternative words or phrases will often help the audience's comprehension. Now and again in an informal presentation the right thing may even be to invite and accept suggestions from the audience – this can help to check understanding and strengthen empathy.

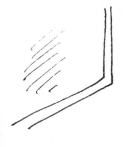

Nerve-reducing tricks

Some speakers have their own nerve-reducing remedies.
Whilst these may not work for everyone, there may be one
which can help us in time of need.

Relaxation
People who have experience of relaxation techniques in
other contexts may wish to try them before speaking. The
easiest for general use are deep breathing or sitting in a
comfortable chair reading a gripping yarn. If we know about
yoga some of its techniques may help. If there is access to a
hot bath that might just do the trick.

Picturing success
Some athletes, such as long or high jumpers, go to great
lengths to visualise success before starting. To imagine in
detail the sensations of making a brilliant presentation while
waiting to start has helped some.

Sharp objects
At least one authority recommends holding some sharp
object so tightly while speaking that it hurts. The idea is that
the slight pain provides a focus for our anxiety and thus frees
us from other more nameless fears. Suitable objects might be
a bunch of keys or the sharp edge of the lectern or ohp.

Picture them in the nude
Anything which helps us to realise that our audience is
made up of ordinary human beings will help to eliminate
unnecessary fear. To imagine the audience unclothed helps
some speakers to do this.

Dutch courage

As with driving, alcohol makes us feel better but perform worse. We should never resort to it as a cure for nerves; rather, we should make sure we avoid it, especially if we are making an after dinner speech. There is, of course, no objection to celebrating our success afterwards.

Setting out our stall

Before getting under way, and preferably before the audience has assembled, we should set out our stall properly. In large and formal presentations, such as a major conference speech, other people will help. But we should never be rushed into starting until we are satisfied everything is in order. In particular, we must always check, *before* we start, that all the equipment we need is ready.

> *Equipment must be*
>
> * Available
> * In the right place
> * Working properly
> * Understandable and controllable

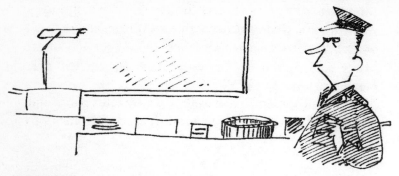

Available
Organisers do not always keep their promises about equipment. As soon as we arrive on site, we should check that what we expect is actually there.

In the right place
It should be placed for us to use easily and without obstructing the line of sight of the audience. We must ensure that there is a sufficiently large surface on which we can place the two piles of not-yet-used and used foils.

Working properly
To test the public address system, video, 35mm slide projectors and ohps before we start will reassure us all is well, or give at least warning of any problems. It is also worth checking that the marker pens write properly, that there is sufficient flipchart paper, or a wiper and the right kind of pens for the whiteboard.

Understandable and controllable
We should try out any operation (including contingencies such as focusing and switching between the bulbs of the ohp) which we may need.

If we plan to rely on someone else's help, for example to change slides, we must ensure that we understand each other clearly before starting.

Final arrangements
With the audience at last in front of us, we must pause and give ourself time to complete our final checks before we give voice:

Final checks

- Rearrange things after the previous speaker
- Put our slides, foils or notes where we want them
- Clip on the tie mike
- Ensure that markers, pointer and a glass of water are to hand
- Draw breath and look up

Presentation

We are on our feet at last and nerves, whilst still making their presence felt, are under control. Seven factors will contribute to our success during the presentation. These are:

> *The factors of success*
>
> - The start
> - Mood
> - The voice
> - The body
> - Aids
> - Timing
> - The conclusion

The start

As with other activities, more than half the battle is getting off to a good start. There are a number of clues to success.

Don't apologise

However we feel, it is wrong to start with an apology. If we expect people to give us their time and attention (and we must) our opening statement must mean 'Listen to me. I have something of interest and importance to you!'. We must never use words which convey the feeling 'I'm not really sure whether I am worth listening to, or whether everything is as it should be, but perhaps you will be prepared to give me a chance'.

This does not mean we should sound brash or overweening, just confident.

Self-introduction
If we have one, it will be the job of the Chair to introduce us. Our responsibility will be to ensure that we talk to whoever is in the chair before the start to agree how he or she should do it and what should (and should not) be said about us.

If we do not have a Chair, we must decide whether it is necessary to introduce ourself. If we are known to all or most of our audience, there is no point in taking time and blunting the impact of our start by indulging in self-introduction.

Mood

Empathy and audience contact
As the presentation moves forward, we will need to make, and keep, contact with our audience, and to mould, understand and respond to their mood. Facial expression, glances exchanged, shuffling of feet, looking at watches, rustling of papers or frequent shifting of position all tell a tale.

Whilst the exact mood we want will depend on our objectives, some factors are important to every presentation. These include:

> ### The right mood
>
> * Professionalism
> * The right degree of formality
> * Controlled enthusiasm
> * Pace and drive
> * Good use of humour
>
> One factor to *avoid* every time is:
>
> * Arrogance

Professionalism
Whatever our other objectives, we will want to create an image of competence and professionalism. If we have prepared well, this should appear naturally, but our manner should reinforce our matter with apparent confidence and control.

The right degree of formality
Our audience analysis (Sunday, p. 9) suggested the degree of formality required. Now we are actually there, we will quickly learn how correct this assessment was and adjust accordingly. Most audiences today prefer a friendly and informal but not unduly familiar style. Unless there are contrary indications, this should be our aim.

Controlled enthusiasm

If we want others to be enthusiastic, we must be enthusiastic ourself. However, it is possible to overdo it; audiences do not like gush.

Pace and drive

As the speaker, we are the locomotive of the presentation; we must keep it moving forward. On the other hand, we must not gabble and rush too fast.

Humour

Natural humorists have a head start as public speakers. Effective use of humour strengthens rapport between speaker and audience, adds enjoyment, makes a presentation memorable, and can disarm tension and disagreement. The witticisms of the cleverest speakers have gone down in history. There are few subjects which cannot benefit from a touch of humour. If we have the gift we should use it.

However, inexpert humour will have the opposite effect. Old, badly-told or unfunny jokes create a barrier between speaker and audience, cause embarrassment and tension, and destroy confidence in the speaker. There is the danger of offending individuals or groups within the audience, particularly in matters of race, religion or politics by including anything which they interpret as critical of themselves or a group to which they belong.

We must therefore know our own ability as a humorist and avoid stretching it too far.

Arrogance

Speakers must respect their audience and make it clear that they do so. Few things put people's back up more quickly than the feeling that the person addressing them is talking down to them. Even though they may have come to learn, the more courtesy and respect we show our audience, the more courtesy and respect they will show to us.

The voice

The voice is the speaker's main weapon (although not the only one; well-chosen and well-used aids will together have at least as much impact). We must use it with skill.

Audibility

The first aim, of course, is to be clearly audible; without this all is lost. The use of PA equipment has been mentioned (Tuesday, p. 46); if it is available we should use it and use it correctly. If there is none, we must project our voice as clearly and loudly as necessary.

To project without shouting or strain takes practice. Hints include:

> *Voice projection*
>
> - Keep your head up
> - Open your mouth wider than in normal speech
> - Use clear consonants
> - Speak more slowly

Interest and meaning

We must consciously emphasise the interest and meaning of what we are saying. We should aim to 'put a shine in our voice'. Meaning is conveyed by using variety of pace, pitch and volume.

Pace is the speed of speaking. We should speed up or slow down as the meaning requires. Fast speaking conveys enthusiasm and urgency, but becomes tiresome if overdone. Slow speaking gives emphasis, but loses attention if used too much. Occasional silence can be very effective to emphasise a point.

Pitch is the musical tone of the voice. This has much the same effect as speed, with the high notes conveying urgency and the low notes emphasis.

Volume is the loudness. We must be audible but avoid shouting. To drop the voice can add significance, if not done too often.

In all three, we must avoid any purely regular variations – over any length of time sing-song rhythms will send the audience to sleep more surely than anything else. Like an actor, we must choose which words to 'hit' – to emphasise – and which we can 'throw away'.

A good exercise is to record a short passage of a top radio announcer or broadcaster, write out what he or she has said, and speak it back into the tape recorder. This will give us a graphic demonstration of the skill with which a professional can convey interest and meaning by the inflections of his voice. The best can make a page of the telephone directory sound like a gripping tale of intrigue, murder and lust.

The body

The body can help or hinder a presentation. Inexperienced speakers feel their body is a problem and become self-conscious about it. Common difficulties include:

> *Using the body*
>
> - Positioning
> - What to do with our hands
> - Eye contact
> - Mannerisms
> - Gestures

Positioning
We must bear several needs in mind, when choosing where
to position ourself:

> ### Position
>
> We must be:
>
> - Visible to all
> - Convenient for our notes
> - Convenient for control of our aids
> - Well placed for the microphone (if
>   used)

If there is a lectern, it is usually best to use it. It provides a
convenient stand for our notes, and may have a light,
controls for the aids and even a clock. Failing this, the
natural place to stand is near the middle of the platform or
speaker's area, with notes on the table. However, if a screen
or flipchart is centrally placed, we must stand to one side
whilst using them and may have to carry our notes. For
right-handed speakers, the left side enables them to use a
pointer and change foils more easily.

It is usually better to stand, even when addressing a small
audience. It is easier to see and be seen and heard, and
shows respect for the audience and the importance of what
we are doing. Sitting is appropriate if our aim is maximum
informality and audience participation; with such objectives,
we might choose to sit on or in front of the speaker's table.

Pacing about by a speaker is distracting. We should have placed our aids as conveniently as possible before starting. Nervous or unnecessary moving about should always be avoided.

What to do with our hands

A lectern is a great help, as hands can be placed easily and naturally on each near corner. The same can be done with an ohp whilst it is switched off. If the table is high, it may be natural to place our hands lightly on it for some of the time. Whilst standing, the most natural place for the hands is relaxed by our sides, unless they are in use for operating visual aids, holding notes or gesturing.

We should avoid putting hands in pockets or clasping them unnaturally to front or back.

Eye contact

Eye contact with individual members of the audience is vital. It has several key functions:

> ### The benefits of eye contact
>
> It:
>
> - Gains and holds attention
> - Establishes rapport
> - Gives feedback

We should spend at least 50% of the time in direct eye-contact with the audience. We should take care to look around everyone, not dwelling too long on individuals unless we are, in fact, speaking to them especially.

In every group there are one or two people who are particularly responsive, indicating their attention by their facial expression and body language. We must avoid giving such people more than their share of eye contact, as we also must avoid undue attention to attractive members of the opposite sex.

Glancing out of the window or at a clock or watch, however briefly, is always noticed and has a negative effect.

Mannerisms

We should not feel that we must stand completely motionless and characterless. However, mannerisms which are repetitive or obviously indicative of tension can be distracting. The commonest of these, which we should take special care to avoid, are:

Mannerisms to avoid

- Swaying from side to side or backwards and forwards
- Fiddling with markers, pointers or glasses
- Placing hands in pockets
- Meaningless repetitive gestures
- Pacing to and fro

Gestures

Some people gesture well naturally. If we have this skill, we should use it. If we do not have it, or are unsure, it is wisest to limit our gestures until we have developed confidence and experience. Weak or repetitive gestures are a distraction.

To learn how skilful our gesturing is, we must have feedback. Video recording is ideal, and the comments of wise and honest friends or colleagues a great help. With these two aids, we can experiment with a range of gestures and practise those which seem most helpful.

Aids

Aids well used can be the making of a presentation, but the same aids badly used can wreck it. Some dos and don'ts of using aids include:

When using aids, do

- Check lines of sight to the edges of the audience
- Use a pointer
- Write first, then read what you have written
- Write from the side
- Write legibly
- Cover items on a list until you reach them
- Remove aids when they are finished with

When using aids, don't

- Block the screen or flipchart
- Speak first and then write what you have spoken
- Speak to the screen or board
- Talk while something is being passed round
- Show one thing and talk about something else
- Give handouts until the end
- Leave an ohp running for long periods

Timing

The feeling that a speaker is unconscious of the passing of time rapidly switches an audience off, especially if there are trains to catch or another speaker is waiting. On the other hand, a speaker who makes clear that he or she will keep to the allotted time inspires confidence.

Some speakers start by taking their watch off (or out), and placing it beside their notes. This allows them to consult it unnoticed, whilst also indicating to all that they intend to control their timekeeping.

The conclusion

The end of a presentation is second only to the start in importance.

Not with a whimper but a bang
It is always right to go out on a high note, and always wrong to tail off into silence or end suddenly and unexpectedly. Whatever else, we should leave no doubt that we have, in fact, come to an end.

Handling questions

Today we will look at how to deal with questions and end with a summary of the week.

No presentation (except a sermon) is complete until the speaker has handled questions from the audience. For some, this is the most frightening part of all, whilst for others it is the part they look forward to most, when they can at last relax and behave naturally. Success at question time depends on three phases:

> *Handling questions*
>
> * Before the presentation
> * At the start of the presentation
> * When questions come

We will look at each in turn.

Before the presentation

The audience analysis (Sunday, p. 9) will have helped us to anticipate questions and identify potential sources of difficulty. Our preparation (Monday, p. 27) should have provided further help. We can do several things:

Before the presentation

- Anticipate questions
- Identify trouble-makers
- Foresee audience tensions
- Prepare reserve material

Anticipate questions

The audience analysis will help us anticipate those aspects of our presentation which will most interest our audience, or are most likely to raise questions. Our understanding of the audience's interests, biasses and existing knowledge will help us to anticipate what sort of questions they are likely to ask, and for what reasons.

Identify trouble-makers

Most audiences do not contain trouble-makers. We should not approach the presentation with the belief that ours will. But we may get clues as to the hobby-horses and preoccupations of individuals who are expected to be present. A friendly warning about Mr X, who 'always asks questions about safety, whatever the subject', or Ms Y, who 'wants to know how single-parent families will be affected', may save us much trouble on the day.

Foresee audience tensions

If the audience is a working group – a Board, committee or management team, for example – any clues we can get about how the members regard each other and get on together may help us to avoid traps. We may learn that Mr Z is unpopular, and others are inclined to reject his view on principle, whilst Mrs W is an unofficial leader, despite not being the top person, and her attitude commands great respect. We may find out that the board is split into two factions, and that whatever one accepts will automatically be rejected by the other – a tricky situation for the speaker, but at least it is better if we know.

Prepare reserve material

When preparing our material, it is often a good idea to prepare extra which we deliberately do not plan to use in the body of the presentation. As stated on Monday (p. 24), we can use it if we find we are short, but better still, hold in anticipation of questions.

At the start of the presentation

We should guide our audience in two ways right at the start.
We can take questions:

How to take questions

- **As they arise**
- **After each section**
- **At the end**

If we have one, it is the job of the Chair to tell the audience
how and when questions will be taken. Before the event
starts, this should have been discussed and agreed. As it
goes on, the Chair should ensure that the arrangement is
kept to. If we have no Chair, we must do the job ourself,
having decided in advance what seems best.

As they arise
This is the best method when we are aiming at informality
and participation. It can be particularly helpful if we are
unsure of the level of knowledge or interests of the audience
and need early feedback to help us pitch the presentation
correctly.

This approach requires good skills in controlling group discussion. If not handled well, it can be distracting both to speaker and audience and can sometimes get out of hand.

After each section
To pause for questions at intervals – for example at the end of the main sections of the presentation – is the best method for a lengthy or complex presentation or lecture. It enables both speaker and audience to check that they are still in touch whilst there is the opportunity to put things right.

At the end
Holding questions until the end is the commonest method. It is essential when speaking to a large audience and on formal occasions. It allows us to develop what we are saying without interruption and is (usually) easier to control. However, it denies us direct feedback on the audience's reactions, and may allow a serious mismatch to develop between what they want and what we are giving them.

When questions come

The degree of formality and the strength of rapport we have with our audience will both affect how and when questions come and how we will be expected to deal with them. Formal presentations will generate formal questions; probably quite long set-pieces to which we will be expected to make set-piece replies. Informal presentations will generate informal questions, comments, interpolations, possibly group discussion. Our job will be to handle this as it comes, to direct it gently but firmly and guide it the way we prefer.

Panic may grip us when at last the moment arrives for
questions. In fact, none may be forthcoming for what seems
like an eternity. To avoid this, some speakers plant one or
two easy questions amongst friends in the audience. There is
nothing wrong with this – it gets the session off to a good
start both for speaker and audience. The Chair may perform
the same office. When the flow has started, the guidelines
listed below will see us through to success:

> ### When questions come
>
> - Listen carefully – right to the end
> - If necessary, repeat or paraphrase
> - Decide why the question has been
>   asked
> - Beware of assumptions
> - Separate the strands
> - Keep cool under fire
> - Never put the questioner down
> - Don't feel you must answer
> - Don't be too long or too short

Listen carefully – right to the end
If we are nervous, we may think we have picked up the
questioner's drift from the first few words, but we may
easily be wrong. One trap is to assume the question is
hostile when it is not.

If necessary, repeat or paraphrase
Repeating or paraphrasing the question is legitimate,
provided it is used sensibly and not too often. Both buy time.

If the questioner is at the front of the audience, repetition may be essential for the benefit of those at the back who have not heard. If we have the least doubt as to the drift of the question, to paraphrase it before answering is far more sensible than risking an answer which is badly off track.

Decide why the question has been asked

Inexperienced speakers always tend to assume that questioners are attacking them or trying to catch them out. Unless the subject is meant to be controversial, the audience have special reason to be hostile, we have upset them, or we have a personal enemy out there, this is unlikely. Most questions at most presentations are asked for quite legitimate reasons:

Questions are asked to

- Obtain additional information
- Clarify doubts
- Support the speaker
- Express interest and appreciation
- Express another point of view
- Make one's mark

Beware of assumptions
The assumptions on which a question is based may be different from ours in some important respect. If the subject is controversial, it will be essential not to allow ourself to be drawn onto false ground and attempt to answer from the wrong starting point. Even in less contentious situations we should always make sure we accept the questioner's presuppositions. If not, a polite statement of our own position will be essential before tackling the actual question.

Separate the strands
Questioners often ask several questions in one, either deliberately whilst they have the floor, or accidentally because they have not thought things through. In either case we must carefully and politely disentangle them before starting to answer any. Naturally, having done so, we will answer the easiest first.

Keep cool under fire
If a question is hostile or personally aimed, we must keep cool. Humour can often defuse an unpleasant situation, as long as we do not resort to sarcasm aimed at the questioner. The best plan is usually simply to ignore the unpleasantness and answer the question as if we had not noticed.

Never put the questioner down
If the question seems silly, ridiculously simple, or if we believe we have fully answered it during the presentation, there is a temptation to say something which makes the questioner look small. This must always be resisted; if it is not, the audience will always side with the questioner against us.

If the question does seem silly or simple, we will do well to keep our feelings to ourself and look for some hidden profundity to help the questioner out. Occasionally, there may actually be some hidden profundity which we have failed to spot. If we sense this, we may decide to explore politely by asking the questioner to explain further.

It is good practice to thank questioners, whether their questions are silly-sounding or not, either in so many words, by implication, or with a smile. In this way both the questioner and the rest of the audience are likely to remain sympathetic to us.

Don't feel you must answer
There is a natural feeling that questions must be answered, but this is not so. There are many options. Depending on circumstances, we can:

Alternatives to a direct answer

- ask for further explanation from the questioner
- throw the question to the audience
- throw the question to a colleague or acknowledged expert who may be present
- throw the question back to the questioner
- admit ignorance (and say we will find out)
- say the answer will come out later in the presentation
- answer a different (and easier) question
- give clues to help the questioner answer the question
- refuse to answer (on grounds of commercial confidentiality, national security or whatever)
- waffle meaninglessly
- turn the situation into a joke
- carry on as if we haven't heard
- walk out
- feign sickness or death

Whilst it is *not* suggested that any or all of these are suitable for general use, it *is* important to remember that there are always alternatives to a direct answer available to us.

Don't be too long or too short
Some speakers tend to use question-time as an opportunity to add large chunks of speech they forgot to deliver, spinning out answers to a great length. This may be a good idea if our aim is to take up as much time as possible and avoid having to answer many questions. Otherwise it is not

sensible, as it will frustrate members of the audience, especially those who are aching to get their question in.

It is not usually polite to answer too briefly either – single word or sentence replies sound curt, even arrogant, as if we can't be bothered to waste time with the questioner. The best length for a reply is, therefore, in between, long enough for us to show we understand and appreciate the point which has been raised, but not so long as to become another speech.

Heckling
There is the danger that members of the audience may take the law into their own hands and heckle or interrupt without invitation. In business presentations such occasions will be rare. However, if we are being consciously controversial or anticipate a hostile audience for other reasons, we must be prepared. If heckling does occur, we are inevitably thrown back on our native wit, aided by suggestions such as those given on page 95. There are several options open to us. In approximate order of effectiveness, these are:

Reactions to heckling

- Make a witty reply
- Give a serious answer
- Carry on as if we have not heard
- Appeal for a fair hearing
- Ask the stewards to throw the heckler out